JIM TURNER

DOUBLE
YOUR TIP$
OR YOUR MONEY BACK

This book is dedicated to my father,
John Joseph Turner

CONTENTS

INTRODUCTION

This book will help you make a lot of money. Read the stories and apply the lessons and you will see results.

It was the summer of 1967 and a popular tune playing on the radio was "Summer in the City" by The Lovin' Spoonful. My friend, Joe Marzano, who had gotten a job at Franksville, a hot dog-only fast-food restaurant on Western Avenue in Chicago Heights, had put in a good word for me, so I was in the back doing all the hard stuff: peeling potatoes, slicing, blanching French fries, and prepping in anticipation of our lunchtime opening. It was my first introduction to the food industry.

We served ten items on a hot dog bun: regular hot dogs, chili dogs, melted cheese dogs, sauerkraut dogs, jumbo dogs, footlong hot dogs, and burger dogs, just to name a few.

A Franksville restaurant at Addison and Harlem avenues on the north side of Chicago. Franksville has expanded its menu to include ribs, chicken, and gyros, since hot dogs by themselves didn't draw enough people.

After that summer ended, I went back to high school and got a job as a bus boy at the Millionaires' Club, helping the waitresses deliver food to customers at a (at the time) high-end restaurant. Every lunch or dinner came with all-you-can-drink cocktails.

Luncheon

11 A.M. — 3 P.M.

To Start a Perfect Luncheon,
Enjoy Your Favorite Cocktails — As Many As You Wish!
This is the Millionaires' Club!

Salad — Garden Fresh Chef's Salad with Choice Of
Our Famous Gourmet Dressings — Or —
Creamy Cole Slaw with Sour Cream Dressing

Entrees

Prime Rib of Beef (Club Specialty) $3.95

New York Cut Boneless Sirloin Steak $3.95

Genuine Prime Steer Filet Mignon $3.95

Roast Sirloin of Beef Au Jus $2.95

Pan Fried Filet of Sole, Tartar Sauce $1.95

Chopped Sirloin Steak (Open Faced Sandwich) $2.50

Barbeque Sirloin of Beef on Toasted Roll $2.50

Broiled African Lobster Tail, Drawn Butter $4.45

Prime Filet Mignon En Brochette $3.95

Baked Shrimp De Johnge En Casserole $3.95

Potato — Millionaires' Supreme Baked or Golden
Brown Steak House Potatoes

Desserts — French Ice Cream, Chocolate Sundae, Or
Our Special Sour Cream Cheese Cake

Beverages — Coffee, Milk, Tea, Sanka or Draft Beer

Dinner

5 P.M. — Midnight

To Start a Perfect Dinner,
Enjoy Your Favorite Cocktails - As Many As You Wish!
This is the Millionaires' Club!

Salad — Garden Fresh Chef's Salad with Choice Of
Our Famous Gourmet Dressings — Or —
Creamy Cole Slaw with Sour Cream Dressing

Entrees

Prime Rib of Beef (Club Specialty) $7.45

Jim Brady Cut (Double Thick) $8.95

Boneless Breast of Chicken Ala Kiev $5.95

New York Cut Boneless Sirloin Steak $7.45

Diamond Jim Cut (Full 1¼ lb.) $8.95

Baked Shrimp De Johnge En Casserole $5.95

Millionaires' Extra Thick Prime Steer Filet Mignon $8.95

U.S. Prime Roast Sirloin of Beef Au Jus $5.95

Broiled African Lobster Tails, Drawn Butter $8.95

Broiled Center Cut Pork Chops (Full Pound) $6.95

Broiled Lake Superior White Fish, Lemon-Butter $6.95

Broiled African Lobster Tail And Filet Mignon
En Brochette $8.95

Broiled Chopped Sirloin Steak $3.95

Potato — Millionaires' Supreme Baked or Golden
Brown Steak House Potatoes

Desserts — French Ice Cream, Chocolate Sundae, Or
Our Special Sour Cream Cheese Cake

Beverages — Coffee, Milk, Tea, Sanka or Draft Beer

A copy of the menu from the Millionaires' Club. Note the pricing and the text below "Luncheon" and "Dinner": "Enjoy Your Favorite Cocktails – As Many as You Wish!"

This is where I first learned to serve customers in a restaurant setting. The wait staff—all women— worked hard, so I helped out when I could. I carried any large trays to the waitresses' tables and then cleaned those off after their customers had left. At the end of the night, the women would chip in to pay me a little extra.

> Every profession has both a science and an art. The science can be taught, and people can be equally good at the science of any profession. The key to differentiate yourself in your profession is to develop the art side, not just the science side.
> – Daniel Burrus, "There Is a Science and an Art to Every Profession"[1]

This book is not a primer on the basics of being a waiter or server (words that will be used interchangeably throughout). Most restaurants already have procedural training for new servers, either written down or through training, maybe even both.

Mostly, this book is about the art of connecting and communicating with the people being served. If you want to be unique in your environment and move up to more exclusive restaurants (where the

---

1   Burrus, Daniel. "There Is a Science and an Art to Every Profession." Burrus Research, January, 2013. https://www. burrus.com/2013/01/there-is-a-science-and-an-art-to-every-profession/

real money is), then look no further. Being a server can even be a springboard to another profession, with any side money used to finance your education or side business.

Being a server has countless advantages: easy entry, easy promotion, easy upward mobility. You don't have to be a server forever, but it's a superb starting place, especially once you see how lacking the competition can be. Yes, some enter this profession only because of its easy entry and the need for immediate cash, but if taken seriously and implemented as both "a science and an art," serving can be the road to phenomenal success and advancement in life.

Being a waiter or waitress in America is a profession that doesn't necessarily require a degree to get started. There are very few places in the world where there is as much real opportunity to advance and change your life situation as there is "in the good old U.S.A." You live in the land of opportunity, a microcosm of success.

And one truly American concept is tipping. To ensure excellent and prompt service, tips can be tacked on to your bill post-meal and/or post-drinks. If your waiter or waitress hasn't taken care of you—is out back smoking, in the kitchen talking, or on their smartphone instead of serving—the thinking goes: If you make me wait and are unfriendly, why should I give you a tip? But if you are pleasant and and don't make me wait, I'm willing to pay more.

I consider myself a good tipper, but sometimes I see servers give up on me and my wife when we order water to start. The servers start thinking about the bill and assume a 20 percent tip will be negligible with our table. So, they stop giving the best service.

My dad used to say, "You are shooting yourself in your own foot." Always give the best service to everyone. Always. Every time you provide skillful service you are positioning yourself for potential marvelous reward. You never know who will sit at one of your tables.

> Do nothing, get nothing.
> Do something, get something.
> Do a lot, get a lot.

If you can give your customers a great experience, then you have made them feel like a winner, and most will want to reward you in some way. *It has now become a mutually beneficial exchange*, a win-win situation. This is the very essence of the free market system: both the customer and provider of the service voluntarily win.

Ray Lazzara (left), who is in charge of food and drinks, and brother John, who runs the theatrical operation, stand outside of their Drury Lane/Martinique complex.

A BIT OF BACKSTORY

The time was the late 1940s. The place was Evergreen Park, Illinois, a southwest suburb surrounded on three sides by the city of Chicago. The Martinique Restaurant was *the* place to go for food and entertainment, eventually opening alongside what became known as the famous Drury Lane Theatre.

The Martinique was a dinner theater, something that doesn't really exist anymore. A dinner theater is a high-end restaurant with a band and live entertainment. Think of the scene in *Goodfellas* where Henry Hill takes his new girlfriend to the Copacabana: high-end food with high-end entertainers, singers, and stand-up comedians.

Anthony De Santis, the founder of Drury Lane, once said of dinner theaters, "They're all just disappearing. One time there were hundreds of them, but now there are only three to five left in the country." The Drury Lane-Martinique complex in Evergreen Park was perhaps the best-known of all dinner theaters in the U.S. Seemingly every well-known, slightly past-his-or-her-prime Hollywood star and recording artist from the past half-century performed: Douglas Fairbanks Jr., Tony Bennett, Cyd Charisse, Claudette Colbert, Phyllis Diller, Julie Newmar, Tony Randall, Mickey Rooney, Lana Turner, Shelley Winters, Gloria Swanson, Ozzie and Harriet. "We booked them all directly," De Santis said in a 2003 article. "The top price was $5,000 per star."[2]

The Drury Lane Theatre was where you went if you were anybody. It was an upscale place with high-quality clientele, most particularly those who visited the Martinique and floor shows.

During the restaurant's heyday in the late 1950s and 1960s, my great-uncle John owned a cab company nearby called Cream Top Cabs that had its main dispatch and office on 95th Street.

---

2   Owens, John. "As final curtain looms, owners review the past." Chicago Tribune, September, 2003. https://www.chicagotribune.com/news/ct-xpm-2003-09-17-0309170041-story.html

Tribune file photo

The Martinique Restaurant was boarded up after an explosion May 30, 1962.

Tribune file photo

The main dining room of the Martinique Restaurant, about 1962.

My dad, also named John, drove a Cream Top cab for his uncle. World War II had recently ended, so there were still a lot of shortages in the U.S., one of them being vehicles.

One of my dad's regular stops was after closing time at the Martinique, where every night he would fill his taxi to the brim with waitresses heading home. Some of these waitresses made as much as $100 in one night, the equivalent of about $1,050 in today's dollars.

How did they make so much in tips?

First off, the Martinique was one of the best places you could work in the entire Chicagoland area, so they got the best waitresses. According to the ones who rode in my dad's taxi every night, other ingredients included a high-priced menu that included alcohol, with most of the clientele moneyed people who could afford high bills. Also, it was an extremely busy place, so bustling that any one waitress could serve dozens of customers in a single night. <u>Most of all, it was because their boss trained his employees in the art and science of customer service.</u> He demanded that they be trained well enough to provide the Martinique's customers with the best service in the world.

He then expected them to perform flawlessly.

Many of the things my dad learned from these waitresses and the Martinique he used as a taxi driver, and then taught me. I wasn't a very good listener when I was younger, but as I got older and learned things the hard way, I shut up and listened. I started to appreciate my father's wisdom, knowledge, understanding, and life experiences. These "tips" are simple but profound.

When my dad retired, a regular part of our day was dining out. He would observe servers and critique them on what they did and didn't do, applying the lessons he learned from the Martinique servers.

These tips will increase your tips and your skills as a server. They will give you the confidence to move up to higher-end restaurants where the real money can be made.

Lesson 1

WHY *DO* PEOPLE GO OUT TO EAT?

If people go to a restaurant just to get food,
why do so few eat alone?

Billy, an 11-year-old, lived in Orange Beach, Alabama, one of the best fishing spots in the U.S. Billy's dad and three uncles would often get together on the weekend and grill out. Billy heard a lot of fish stories at these backyard cookouts.

As with all young boys, he dreamed of the day he could tell his own fish story in front of his dad, uncles, and grandpa. It was summertime, and Billy lived within walking distance of an assortment of piers, wharfs, and fishing spots. There was plenty of fishing equipment at Billy's home—some he could use, some only for his dad, uncles, and grandfather. Billy would get up every day and, after finishing his chores, head out to fish.

Billy didn't really know much about fishing, but that didn't matter to him. How hard could it be? His dad, uncles, and grandpa all had grand stories about catching fish. It was simple: All you had to do was bait a rod and throw the line into the water, then boom! A fish. At least that's what Billy thought. He just wanted to catch a really big one so he could tell a fish story, too.

Every day, Billy went fishing, but he wasn't catching any, or at least not one big enough to bring home or tell a story about to his dad, uncles, or grandpa. Billy was determined. He went fishing every day. After several weeks, he started to get discouraged. He started to internalize this discouragement, thinking there was something terribly wrong with himself. The more he failed to catch a fish, the more he believed himself a failure.

About halfway through the summer, Billy stopped going fishing. He knew some people could catch fish … just not him. Then one day, his grandpa came to visit from out of town. He was retired and had plenty of time on his hands, so he asked Billy if he wanted to go fishing. Billy hesitated in his answer. His grandpa, being a perceptive man, knew something was wrong, so Billy told his grandpa about his inability to catch fish. His grandpa told Billy that fishing looked easy, but it actually required a lot of skill. Since his grandpa would be in town for three months, he could teach Billy how to fish.

So, Billy and his grandpa went fishing every day. About one week before summer would be over, Billy caught three very big fish. That weekend, Billy was able to tell his own fish story to his dad, uncles, and grandpa.

The same is true about most of life. Many things look and seem easy, but they usually aren't. People get discouraged and quit. Many take it personally and believe there's something wrong with themselves or with the profession or activity they're trying. Sometimes people simply aren't suited for a job and activity, but more often, it's because a person hasn't been given the right kind of training.

The same is true for a server. Some basics need to be internalized, and having a good understanding of why people go out to eat is the foundation of becoming a good server.

When you first serve a customer, think about why they came to the restaurant and how you can help them accomplish that goal. Most people don't go just to get food. They could be getting together with a friend, going on a date or anniversary, celebrating an event, or socializing with a client or boss. Tourists might want to know the lay of the land.

So, what is it essentially that most of your customers want? First, they want to socialize. Sure, they want good food and drinks, too, but they want to focus on each other or the entertainment (if any).

Your job is to make that happen. If you can, your tips will skyrocket, and when people return, they'll ask specifically for you. <u>Repeat business is one of the keys to success.</u> The server's job, if he or she is smart and wants more tips, is to see what the customer wants and then give that to him or her.

What many people need is someone like Billy's grandpa: someone who can teach them, who can help them understand what they need to learn, who can help them understand not only the basics but some tried-and-true skills. Being a successful server requires training, which few restaurant owners invest in. This book will help you develop an understanding and broaden your skills.

Just like Billy, most wait staff don't think being a server requires that much skill. But being aware of *why* people go out to eat is especially important. *You have to understand your customer if you are going to serve them well.*

Think of it like dancing: When you dance, you do so to the beat of the music. If you're offbeat, your dancing reflects that. In the same way, understanding *why* customers go out to eat should become second nature. You need to be more than an order-taker and food delivery person.

Lesson 2

WAIT <u>IS</u> A
FOUR-LETTER WORD

"BIG QUESTION"

When
you "wait"
for a waiter
in a restaurant,
aren't you a waiter?

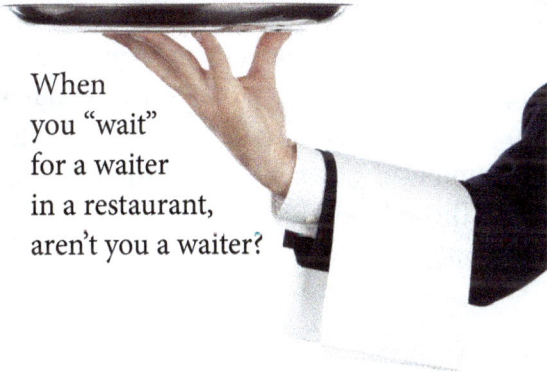

Let's say a couple meets another couple for dinner. Getting drinks ordered is the first order of business—the table's first connection with the server—but you haven't stopped by yet. Most party members are just plain thirsty, but one of them needs to down some medication before eating. It has become a stressful waiting game for the unofficial "leader" who feels it is his or her unofficial task to make sure the other diners at the table get what they need.

You know they've been seated at your table. You think to yourself, "Surely they can see how busy I am. I'll get to them as soon as I can, but it's first-come, first-served. If I don't look at them, they won't flag me and I can take care of these other customers."

But the first thing your new guests are thinking is, "Where is our server? Who is our server? Does he/she know we are here? When will he/she be coming to our table to get this evening started?" The relationship starts off with immediate disappointment.

There are two moments when diners are the most impatient at a restaurant: when they've just arrived and when they're ready to leave.

Let's talk about the key word in this scenario: "Wait." Do you like to wait? Or know anyone who likes to? Don't let the first thing you serve your new customers be "wait." Think of it instead as a four-letter word to avoid.

You may be thinking: "I have ten tables to serve. Some of my customers will *have* to wait." That's where you're making your first mistake.

The diners just want to know you see them and will be attending to them soon. *"Soon" is a better four-letter word than "wait."* Everyone knows you have other tables to take care of.

So, how do you resolve this? That brings us to your next lesson.

Lesson 3

NONVERBAL COMMUNICATION

Look at every one of your customers every time
you enter or leave the dining floor.
Discipline yourself to do this every time.

Many servers have intentional blinders on: they avoid looking at the customer because they're afraid he or she will want immediate attention when it's not possible to do so. The issue is, most customers realize you can't help them immediately; they just want you to acknowledge that they need something *soon*. If you don't look, they must continue to *wait*. *Look* at your tables every so often and use hand signals or head movements to communicate.

This is one of the most important things you need to learn and more importantly do: communicate with the customer. Someone at the table won't be able to socialize until they've ensured the table is being taken care of, so acknowledging the customer in some small way allows everyone to relax, know that you are aware they are there, and that you will be attending to them soon. Simple eye contact along with a nod often suffices.

Nonverbal communication is one of your most powerful and effective tools as a server. It allows you to be transported across the room and back in less than a second. (And you thought you could only be in one place at a time!)

Imagine you usually serve six tables, but someone doesn't show up for work. So now you're overseeing ten or more tables, each with two to four people. That's roughly twenty to forty people to serve *at the same time*, and they all need and want something, with only you to meet their needs and wants.

Here's where nonverbal communication comes into play: make eye contact with someone at every table, give them a nod with your head, and, if you aren't holding a food tray, a hand gesture in less than two seconds. If you average two to three seconds to gesture at each table, that's only half a minute to acknowledge every table under your purview.

So, even if you haven't spoken to your new customers yet, they can focus on socializing and enjoying themselves because of *you*.

Let's take the situation a step further. Wouldn't it be nice if you knew in advance everything each customer would need, want, and desire? But each one could need a refill, an additional napkin, new silverware, to complain about the food, help with spillage … the list goes on.

Each one of these wants, needs, and desires is an opportunity to ensure your customer is satisfied.

So, every time you're in the dining area, make eye contact, nod your head, and make a hand gesture with every single table. If they don't need your attention, they won't look at you. *Always be on the lookout.*

Recognizing the power and effectiveness of eye contact and body gestures will increase your customers' satisfaction—along with your tips.

Lesson 4

WHEN TO TALK ... OR NOT

There is
"a time to be silent and a time to speak."
— Ecclesiastes 3:7 NIV

According to the waitresses my dad taxied home in the 1940s and 1950s, the Martinique's manager was tough but fair. He knew that if he took care of his customers, they'd be back, and his primary tool for ensuring that was excellent service. He spent a lot of time training and supervising the waitresses, and most of them knew they made more money each night because of his diligence.

One of the primary methods they were taught was to let the customer lead the conversation. Some customers want to talk as little as possible, while others talk up a storm.

So, my dad used it in his work as a cab driver. When he'd pick up a fare, he'd look and listen. If his fare wanted to talk, he'd talk; if his fare didn't, neither would my dad. He said his tips went up noticeably.

Think of it as couple's dancing, where there's a "leader" and a "follower," or an orchestra, when the musicians follow the cues of the conductor. In a service situation, *the customer is the lead and the server is the follower*, meaning it's up to the customer to let you know how much he or she wants to talk.

When you approach a table, *allow them to let you know when to talk*. If they're talking with each other, wait until they stop and look at you. If they don't acknowledge you, back up and move on to another table.

The better you learn to read signals from your customers, the bigger the tips.

Now look at the picture below. To talk or not to talk?

Since neither diner appears to be looking at the waiter, the answer is not to talk. The waiter should wait for someone to look at him; otherwise, he can leave behind their meals and move on since the table knows he's there. Don't talk. Don't interrupt. Serve.

What about the picture below? To talk or not to talk?

The customers are all engaging with the waitress, so it's the perfect time to talk. *But remember to follow the customers' lead*. If they want to talk a lot, then talk a lot. If you sense they don't want to talk a lot, then speak as little as possible. Let the customers drive the conversation with their words and body language.

**Learn how and when to talk
and your tips will skyrocket.**

Lesson 5

NEVER INTERRUPT

One time, my wife and I were out to dinner with another couple. The server had so far been fantastic. The food plates had been cleared and we were enjoying some intense conversation with the other couple. The server walked up and asked if there was anything else we wanted. The problem was, she had interrupted us in the middle of talking, and I subsequently forgot about what we had been conversing. The server had good intentions, but the mood had been broken.

If your customers are talking, approach the table or barstools where they're sitting (but without getting too close) and wait for acknowledgment. Don't say anything. They see you. They feel you. If they want to talk to you, they will. But if they don't, quietly back away and, if they make eye contact, give a hand signal to let them know you've acknowledged this. Remember the TIPS.

Don't interrupt and then hope for a bigger tip. To the customer, that's saying, "I have a lot of customers. Can you please stop what you are doing so I can move on to my other tables?" In this case, you're not serving the customer; you're undermining his or her purpose for coming out to dine.

Pay attention to your customer. *Allow* your presence to be felt. If the customer doesn't look at you or talk to you, move on. Read his or her body language to know when it's time to stop by.

This is not the time to come to the table and ask, "Do you need anything?"

Lesson 6

TABLE ETIQUETTE

The greatest among you will be your servant.
— Matthew 23:11 NIV

Imagine you awaken from an afternoon nap to sixteenth-century England. You're first cousin to the British royal family, and one of the servants informs you dinner will be served in the downstairs dining room.

You head downstairs and are escorted to your place at the table, the servant gently pushing in the chair as you sit down. As the servants portion out the plates, all on the left side, the family members continue talking to each other, with no one acknowledging the serving staff.

Everything just happens with little verbal communication. As each family member finishes off a course, you notice them placing their cutlery in different places and in different ways, signaling to the servants to remove and replace their plate. As the meal ends, the table is cleared and the appropriate dessert plates delivered.

Was serving ever really that elaborate? Do people ever do that today?

Who Uses Table Etiquette Anyway?

One of the unique things about America is our somewhat impudent sense that in America, no one is better than anyone else. America is regarded as the land of equal opportunity, since it's in many ways a land of immigrants. Yes, most people nowadays are born and raised here, but in almost all instances, they hail from immigrants, even generations back.

Almost none of these immigrants were rich or royalty in their home countries; instead, they were a variety of poor and middle-class individuals that moved to America, which is one reason the signaling system generally isn't practiced in America except in high-end restaurants or homes.

On top of that, Americans are traditionally more casual in their lives. When it comes to using, knowing, and understanding table etiquette, Americans adopt a laidback attitude.

"So, if Americans traditionally don't use table etiquette, who cares?" you might ask. Well, a lot more people than you think. As Americans begin to move up socially and financially, they absorb better table etiquette so they don't look or act "low-class"—especially if that's how they grew up. Professionals who want to ascend the career ladder hope to impress their bosses and customers at work lunches and dinners. The best private schools actually train students in etiquette. And foreign tourists may use fine etiquette naturally.

Any customer that knows this system recognizes when a server responds to it. Knowing these signals not only impresses your customers, but will also be something you need to know as you move on to better restaurants—and those are where the money is. The better you serve and provide service to others, the more you can prosper. Keeping your customers happy will pay great dividends.

American and Continental Style

There are two styles of table etiquette to know: American and continental (also called European). The American style is (naturally) used by North Americans and Canadians, while the continental style is practiced by people the world over, especially Europeans and South and Central Americans.

There are a lot of parts and pieces to proper table etiquette, but fortunately there are only a few that servers need to know and understand, specifically non-distracting signals that diners can send to their *attentive* server.

Below are some cutlery positions to keep in mind.

American style —
"I'm still eating" position

American style —
"I'm finished" position

Continental style —
"I'm still eating" position

Continental style —
"I'm finished" position

(note that the fork tines are placed down on both of these)

Napkins also can be used to strategeous advantage.

"I'm still eating" napkin position

"I'm finished" napkin position

Clearing the Table

So, when is the proper time to remove customers' plates and utensils?

If you remove someone's plate too early, those at the table who are still finishing their meal may think, "I must be eating too slowly. I should hurry up." Plus, the person who has finished may want to use the plate to sample a portion of their significant other's or tablemates' food.

Don't remove a plate unless the customer signals you with either a finished code or verbal/nonverbal consent, and make sure any glass is completely empty before removing it. When in doubt, ask (but don't interrupt!).

Lesson 7

WAYS TO COMMUNICATE

M y wife, Katia, and I went out one night to a restaurant. Our normal style with servers is to be personable and friendly, so we asked our server a few personal questions. "How long have you worked here?" we queried. "Six years," our server responded. No smile. No enthusiasm. This continued throughout the night. Some will say, "They didn't have to be friendly, just professional," and they'd be right. But it lessened how much I wanted to tip over the usual 15 percent.

You don't have to go above and beyond in giving the customer everything he or she wants, but doing so definitely garners more tips. As my dad used to say, "You can be right, but don't be dead right."

My dad once told me that one of the lessons he internalized from the waitresses he drove home was to be discerning. When he would pick up a new ride in his cab, he knew that how and when he talked to this new rider would affect the tips he'd get. So, he'd study the customer to determine what he or she wanted. If the customer wanted to talk, my dad would talk. If the customer didn't, he wouldn't. And his tips went up.

Method of Communication

Some of your customers are going to want you to act like a servant and maintain a distant, non-personal attitude. This can be difficult for anyone raised in America, since most of us are not naturally disposed to think like followers. The American line of thinking is, "Nobody is better than anyone else."

However, if you're more interested in tips than your pride, you'll pay attention and defer to the customers' way of thinking. They didn't come here to see you; they came to be with the people they're seated with and to enjoy some good food and drinks. You as their server are strictly to deliver these things.

Some customers may not want to get too friendly or personal with you. Others don't mind you being friendly and are more likely to look at you and smile often, even ask you some personal questions. Still others could be somewhere in the middle: they may want you to be professional but at the same time personable about it.

Let the customers lead. If they're somewhere in the middle, don't get too personal too quickly. If they want distance, don't get upset; just serve them well. Do so, and each type should tip accordingly.

Now, some servers may say, "This is my style. This is the way I treat every customer." You can of course continue to do so, but just be prepared for a lower tip.

Remember, give your customers what they want and they will give you what you want: *tips*.

Lesson 8

GET ON THE FLOOR

One night, my wife and I dined at a restaurant where the waitress came to our table right away. She took our drink order and came back quickly to take our food order, but we weren't yet ready, even after she had returned a couple of times. At last, we decided on what we wanted. We waited and waited. Our waitress had disappeared. Finally, I explored the bar area to see if I could find our waitress, then noticed a side door leading out. There, I found our waitress on a smoke break and told her we were ready to order. Embarrassed, she quickly came to our table. Her performance after that was stupendous, and we ending up giving her a 20 percent tip. She had redeemed herself after almost losing a bigger tip.

Don't disappear on your customers. It can and will cost you money. Your customers constantly have needs: another napkin, another drink, another knife, some salt and pepper, some ketchup, the check ... the list goes on. Don't make your customers wait to get any of these things. You must be on the floor as much as possible. Be there. Be available. Be visible.

There is a correlation between what you do and what you receive. This is key to you making progress, not just as a server, but also in life. "Give, and it will be given to you. A good measure, pressed down, shaken together and running over, will be poured into your lap. For with the measure you use, it will be measured to you" (Luke 6:38 NIV). This is the foundation of a mutually beneficial exchange: supplying something of value to a customer that results in a corresponding monetary acknowledgment.

> There is a correlation between what you do and what you receive. This is key to you making progress, not just as a server, but also in life.

When you are not paying attention to your customers, you are not giving them what they want and need. Don't use your cellphone when you're working, or at least not where customers can see you. If you want to double your tips, you need to be on the floor where you can see your customers and they can see you. You should be watching them, making eye contact, and making sure they are not waiting on *you*. You don't have to run; you just have to look and signal, then attend.

Lesson 9

MAKING MEMORIES

Not long ago, I received a phone call from a friend from high school about our fiftieth reunion. Reunions are nostalgia-laden trips down memory lane that let you return to the area where you grew up. I planned not only on catching up with old friends but downing my favorite Chicago-land foods.

My favorite eatery, the Easy Snack in Chicago Heights, had closed years ago, but my friends told me about a restaurant called Enzo's only a few blocks over from the old Easy Snack location. The experience was memorable.

The first things I *saw* when entering were signs for my two favorite Chicago-famous foods:

The Chicago hot dog

An Italian roast beef sandwich

The next thing that hit me was the *smell* of the food cooking in the kitchen and then, after ordering, the *taste.* Those senses brought back memory after memory of being a teenager and young adult growing up in Park Forest and Chicago Heights.

The three things that both created and brought back memories were the *sights, smells, and tastes* of this unique Chicago cuisine. Have you ever experienced that? A picture on TV or your computer that reminded you of home. The smell of a certain food or drink reminiscent of a favorite restaurant. A certain dessert that harked back to Grandma's apple pie. Those memories are embedded with the perceptions we had in that moment.

Can you as a server help a customer create a unique and great memory? Yes, you can. This is where the actual art form of being a server is paramount. A server can help his or her customer experience some great sights, smells, and tastes, especially after dinner, depending on what type of drink and/or dessert is recommended.

If your customer is celebrating something, help him or her discover a delightful dessert or cocktail to help remember this night.

> Can you as a server help a customer create a unique and great memory? Yes, you can.

According to Wikipedia: "Dessert is a course that concludes a meal. The course consists of sweet foods, such as candy, and possibly a beverage such as dessert wine and liqueur.... The term *dessert* can apply to many sweets, such as biscuits, cakes, cookies, custards, gelatins, ice creams, pastries, pies, puddings, macaroons, sweet soups, tarts, and fruit salad."[3]

---

3   "Dessert." Wikipedia, October, 2023. https://en.wikipe-

Culturally in America, dessert is looked at in two ways: as a time to enjoy something sweet (with the exception of coffee) or to aid in the digestion of food. As a server, you can suggest pairings that accomplish both. The post-dinner period is a time when many waiters and waitresses miss an opportunity to help their customers make the meal unique, memorable, and lasting. *Now is the time for some role reversal, when it's your turn to help lead customers to a lasting impression that can amass higher tips.*

Many times, people go to a restaurant to celebrate. It may be a birthday, an anniversary, Valentine's Day, the consummation of a great business deal, a family reunion, etc. You, as the server, are helping that celebration happen. Mention to your customers some great after-dinner options when taking their drink or food order. Get them thinking about dessert and after-dinner drinks to make this night special.

For example, some restaurants have a large array of coffees, while others offer an unbelievable dessert menu or boast an incredible bar with a variety of specialty dessert cocktails. Mention any after-dinner delights as soon as you can, preferably

dia.org/wiki/Dessert

while taking their drink order or, if the customer looks like he or she wants to talk, when you bring out the party's order.

Like all good business transactions, this is a mutually beneficial exchange: a unique experience for them, larger tips for you.

After-Dinner Drinks

If you work in a restaurant with a bar, you need to know about drinks, especially after-dinner ones. Although people usually know what type they're going to order before dinner, *after dinner* is different. Try to persuade your restaurant manager or bartender to let you sample one of each drink so you can better understand how each type can help cap off a great meal.

Help your customers experience an after-dinner delight. This may take some salesmanship, but suggest an after-dinner coffee, wine, or whiskey as something unique and different to lubricate the party's conversation. Mentioning it earlier in the meal may help them decide on something by the time you ask again or, if they don't know much about after-dinner drinks, be open to suggestions.

Pairing

Pairing is combining the right drink with the right food. Properly doing so requires vast experience, and even though this isn't a book about pairing, understanding what it is, is critically important.

Pairing is highly subjective, with the bottom line being the customer's personal preference. However, understanding the fundamentals can still be extremely helpful. The best thing is you only have to learn what to pair with what you serve at your restaurant.

My family is a good example of personal preference being outside the norm. Red wine, according to experts, should be served cool between 62 and 68 degrees. My dad, however, liked red wine right out of the refrigerator at about 40 degrees. My ex-mother-in-law liked to put ice cubes in her Chardonnay, which often dilutes the flavor. The bottom line is, people can drink whatever they like the way they like it with anything they like.

Caution Ahead

When it comes to recommending a drink, make sure it's not more than your customer wants to spend. Many people are unfamiliar with how expensive after-dinner drinks can get. Memorize the menu or check with management or the bartender so you know the price of any drinks before recommending them. If the customer wants a higher-priced drink, he or she typically will request a particular brand.

Coffee

Let's start off with coffee. Some people don't drink alcohol or are on strict diets that don't allow for desserts, but coffee that can possibly pair with dessert is a good place to start. Hopefully your restaurant offers more than a standard cup of joe. Below is a list of alcoholic and non-alcoholic coffees you can suggest. See if your bartender can make these or mock up your own printed list to offer to customers if the bartender has the ingredients and the willingness to make them.

Remember, offer dessert and/or after-dinner drink options *before* you bring by the check.

Coffee (non-alcoholic)
- Standard
- Cappuccino
- Café latte
- Espresso
- Double espresso

Coffee (alcoholic)
- Spanish coffee (add brandy)
- Mexican coffee (add Kahlua)
- Italian coffee (add Amaretto)
- Irish coffee (add Jameson Irish Whiskey)
- French coffee (add Grand Marnier)
- Keoke coffee (add Kahlua and brandy)
- Mudslide coffee (add Baileys and Kahlua)

- Russian coffee (add Frangelico and vodka)
- Jamaican coffee (add Myers's Original Dark Rum and Tia Maria)

Cocktails

The **Brandy Alexander** is made with Crème de Cacao, a chocolate liqueur that combines cream and cognac. A favorite of John Lennon, it was once described by the former Beatle as tasting like a milkshake.

The **White Russian**, a chocolate mocha-like drink with cream, mixes vodka with either coffee liqueur (typically Kahlua) or dark Crème de Cacao for a richer chocolate flavor.

A beautiful White Russian

The **Grasshopper** doesn't have much of a kick. Instead, it tastes like Thin Mints or Peppermint Patties converted into liquid form.

Wines

Alcoholic beverages have been consumed since at least the time of Noah, who overindulged following the flood (see Genesis 9:21). Wines in particular have immense variety and tastes. Do your own homework on the subject: watch YouTube or TikTok videos, browse the internet, join a wine appreciation club, talk to the salespeople in your local liquor store, buy or borrow a book about drinks, etc. Become knowledgeable on the subject.

Sparkling Wines

A sparkling wine is any kind that has bubbles, denoting its carbonation. The term *Champagne* is used only if it hails from the Champagne wine region in France (*Prosecco* if it comes

from the so-named region in Italy). Sparkling wines can be served before, during, or after a meal, per the diner's preference.

Port Wines

Port wine—fortified with a distilled spirit, most commonly brandy—is considered a digestif and can be imbibed on its own or with a dessert.

Ruby port tastes fruitily sweet and pairs well with darker/sweeter chocolate desserts and tart fruits such as blueberries or blackberries.

Tawny port tastes more complex and is offered in a variety of flavors, such as hazelnut, caramel, and raspberry. Its bolder taste pairs well with lighter chocolate or caramel desserts and fruits such as pears, figs, and apples. It also goes great with milky desserts such as cheesecake.

Cordials (aka Liqueurs)

Liqueurs, which often make up part of after-dinner cocktails, are excellent on their own as a dessert drink. You can even sip them alongside a cup of coffee. They can be sipped without ice ("neat") or with ice ("on the rocks"). Below are the most common, though there are hundreds more available:

- Kahlua: a sweet and strong-tasting coffee flavor
- Baileys Original Irish Cream: creamy and lightly coffee-flavored with a hint of chocolate
- Disaronno: a sweet, almond-like taste with a hint of cherry
- Frangelico: hazelnut-like with a hint of vanilla and chocolate
- Grand Marnier: a deep, complex orange taste with oak and vanilla tones
- Cointreau: an intense orange flavor that still feels light and simple thanks to a balance of spices
- Drambuie: similar to sweetened scotch, with honey, cloves, and fruity floral notes
- Galliano: a predominantly vanilla favor, tinged with shades of citrus and wood
- B&B (Bénédictine and Brandy): honey- and licorice-like, with notes of spices such as cinnamon, peppermint, mint, and nutmeg

Brandy

Brandy is a distilled liquor made from fermented fruit juice, most commonly grapes, with the most renowned being cognac from the Cognac region of southwest France. Its high proof helps settle stomachs, so suggesting it as an after-dinner drink is ideal. Refer to your restaurant's drink menu, bartender, and manager to see what's available.

Whisk(e)ys

Whiskey (spelled "whisky" in Scotland and Canada) is produced from fermented cereal grain mash (e.g., corn, rye, wheat) and aged in barrels. Scotch whisky, according to U.S. regulations, must be entirely produced and bottled in Scotland to be deemed scotch, while bourbon must be produced entirely in the U.S. using a sour mash process (i.e., fermented with yeast) consisting of at least 51 percent corn mash. In addition, U.S. regulations stipulate that rye whiskeys be yielded from a mash that is at least 51 percent rye. Like brandy, whiskey's high proof helps break down food after a long meal, which makes it an outstanding digestif.

Lesson 10

FROM BEGINNING TO END

*T*wo men met at an investment seminar. During a short break, they talked for a few minutes. The younger of the two sold cleaning supplies for keeping trucks clean, while the other owned a trucking company. Both hit it off and talked over the next few breaks. At the end of the day, the younger salesman suggested they meet for coffee to discuss potential investment in the trucking company, so they agreed to meet at nine the following morning at a nearby restaurant.

The next day, the older of the two arrived at about 8:55 a.m. When the other hadn't arrived by 9:15 a.m., he decided to give him a call.

The salesman picked up on the first ring. "You're late!" the older man said in a friendly manner. "Did I come at the wrong time?"

"No," the salesman said. "I'm still at my office. I didn't know if you were going to show up, but I figured you'd give me a call if you did. Give me twenty minutes and I'll be there."

The older gentleman, unhappy, said, "If that's the kind of service I can expect doing business with you, I'd like to cut off our business relationship right now."

This is a great example of how something small but important can sour a potential relationship.

Similarly, one of the most important times in a diner's experience is the beginning of the meal after they are seated. Giving your customer a good first impression will help cover any future shortcomings.

As a server, you don't necessarily have control over how long a customer waits before he or she gets seated in your serving area; that's up to the host or hostess. But once customers are seated in your serving area, they will want to know as soon as possible that their server knows they are there and that they will be attended to shortly.

As soon as you spot new customers in your area, communicate, even if you're carrying a tray of food to another customer. Make eye contact if possible. Smile and nod your head. Give them an acknowledgment that you know they are there.

Then, get to them as soon as possible. Some people suggest that you should get to their table within a minute, but that isn't always possible. Nonverbal communication extends that timetable and allows the customers to relax knowing you have seen and acknowledged them.

When you first approach their table, be pleasant, make eye contact, and tell them your name. Be personable.

Then ask them what they would like to drink. Even better, ask them if they would like something from the bar. This is your opportunity to lead them to an incredible experience. Some people know exactly what they want to drink, while others are open to suggestions. Be creative. If they hesitate, suggest a house specialty or something a little out of the norm. In any case, get any drink orders into the bar and out to your customers promptly.

Some servers or restaurants bring water when they first visit a new customers' table. Don't, if you are free to do this differently; this just causes another delay, especially for those customers who want their water in a specific way (without ice, with lemon, sparkling water, etc.).

Oftentimes, the bar is understaffed or overly busy, so build on your relationship with whoever is making drinks. Having a good relationship with the bartender puts your tables' drinks at the head of the queue. Do this with the chef as well. When they take care of you, don't forget to take care of them with a little of your tips. This goes a long, long way.

When you bring your customers their first drinks, place them to the right of the customer.

Don't touch the top part of the glass; instead, handle the stem or bottom.

Now may be a good time to bring out the food and drink menu. It may also be a good time to ask if they are interested in ordering an appetizer or interject something about post-meal options. Plant a seed in their minds about dessert and after-dinner drinks. Your table will probably need some time to look at the menu, but regulars may be ready to order. In any case, let them take their time. Be attentive on the floor after handing out the menu, and make sure you know your restaurant's typical offerings and specials to help answer any questions.

When they are ready to order, it's typical to take orders from ladies first if they're ready, and from one of the men if they're not. If any children are present, take their order as quickly as possible to stave off childish impatience.

Most of all, use discernment in distinguishing the table's tempo. Some evening diners want to draw out the dining experience, while others may be in a hurry. If you keep an attentive eye on your tables, you should know who is looking for you and expecting you. If you're unable to attend to them yet, politely ask them if you could come back shortly. Most people will understand, especially if you continue to acknowledge them.

The Ending

It takes twenty years to build a reputation and five minutes to ruin it. If you think about that, you'll do things differently.[4]
— Warren Buffett

The second most important time in a customers' dining experience is near the end of your customers' meal.

The big question is, when do you present the check? The answer? It depends on which meal you are serving: breakfast, lunch, or dinner.

Breakfast

At breakfast, the check always is delivered face-down after the main course has been delivered to the customer. Breakfast is not followed by dessert,

---

4   "A Quote by Warren Buffet." Goodreads.com, 2023. https://www.goodreads.com/quotes/618606-it-takes-20-years-to-build-a-reputation-and-five

so leave the check for the customer so they can leave when ready.

Lunch

People at lunch oftentimes are on break from work. They may have a strict one-hour limit in getting to the restaurant, eating, and getting back to work. After the main course, offer dessert and coffee. If they decline, deliver the check. If they take dessert and coffee, deliver the check after they finish their dessert with a final coffee refill.

Dinner

Dinnertime is by far the hardest time to determine when to present the bill. You don't want to rush the customer out the door. Some may want more to drink or an after-dinner offering. Make a pitch if you feel there might be an opening, but don't bring the check before doing so unless requested.

Monitor you customers closely near the end of the meal. If it looks like they are ready to leave, you can go ahead and ask them if they would like their check, but keep in mind that doing so too early can be interpreted poorly. Be close enough that they can signal you for the check, and present it with a thank-you as your last service to those customers. Help them remember you did a tip-worthy job.

When someone pays in cash, don't ask if he or she wants any change; instead, make sure to tell him or her you will bring back change. Doing the former can be regarded as manipulative.

Above all, give your best service at any and all times. You want to start and end the night by impressing your customers. It will pay dividends—I mean tips.

Lesson 11

COOPERATION & TEAMWORK

Most of this book is about what to do and not to do, but as with almost any job, you can't do it by yourself. You are dependent on too many people, be it the host or hostess, cook, bartender, manager, other servers, etc. You need to learn how to get them on your side and helping you whenever and wherever they can.

Let's say the host or the hostess doesn't like you. Since he or she is the one who decides who is going to sit at what table in the restaurant, he or she has the power to seat the worst people in your section and the best people in another server's section. This could lead to you making less money in tips every night.

Same with the chef. If you and the chef have problems, your customers might be getting their food cooked at the end of the queue.

Remember, you're part of a team working toward the same goal. A smart server will maintain a healthy and functioning working relationship with their colleagues.

How to Influence People

Some people are naturals at interacting with people. Some have the personality, looks, or connections to get the kind of cooperation they need in a restaurant environment. However, it all begins and ends with treating people right—the Golden Rule.

Many years ago, I was involved in a Christian ministry for people who had serious drug problems, most often heroin. The leader and founder of this ministry, Gene Dawson, taught the staff that the people there did not care one whit about your position. In fact, they might dislike you just because you had some form of formal authority.

As a private nonprofit and self-supporting ministry, we operated thrift stores, gas stations, and upholstery shops. Working in these businesses was part of a person's rehabilitation, so we needed their cooperation. Gene told us, "If people know and think you care about them and treat them right, they are usually willing to do most anything you ask them to." This spoke very powerfully to me.

People don't trust anyone who they think won't act in their best interests. The people you trust are people you know and who care about you. With informal authority, people voluntarily give you their cooperation. The question is, can anyone learn to do that? If you are a natural with relationships, it will probably be easy, but even if you're not, you can still learn.

Sometimes the simplest things escape us. Sometimes we let our circumstances dominate our life. Just look at the profound insight Jesus gave two thousand years ago: "So whatever you wish that others would do to you, do also to them" (Matt. 7:12 ESV).

Say thanks to people anytime you can. My wife, Katia, does this, and it is truly amazing the effect it has on me. It humbles and delights me. It also motivates me to treat her even better.

In the same vein, thank the host or hostess for seating people in your area. Thank the chef or bartender for getting your orders out so quickly. They will appreciate it more than you know.

Look people in the eye and use their name when talking to them. Show people respect and kindness. Say nice things and pay compliments. As my dad used to tell me, "You can catch more bees with honey than with vinegar." You can sway people's behavior and get the cooperation you need to be successful in taking care of your customer. So, vinegar or honey? Which one do you think works best?

However, that doesn't mean you need to be a pushover—don't let *anyone* disrespect you. But how you respond to disrespect should be done strategically, depending on who's doing it and when and where it's being done.

Picture an upscale party with some VIP attendees. Most go to meet and greet people or schmooze their way up the social or corporate ladder, but if you're not above them on the ladder, you're invisible. These kinds of people will walk right by, avoiding looking at you or saying hi. When this happens, I usually say something like, "What, you aren't even going to say hi?" Nearly every time, they recognize they have been rude, and by standing up for myself like this, I ensure they almost always say hi to me in the future. Be nice but assertive when combatting disrespect and choose the right time and place to do so.

Financial Influence

Financial influence, on the other hand, is a little more complicated. First, I recommend you already be working in a higher-end restaurant with a minimum cost of $50 a plate. To give your customers the best service possible, you need the cooperation of the chef, bartender, and host or hostess. When you're making this kind of money, it pays to give a tip of your own when the tip is due.

For example, if the chef is making sure your orders don't get pushed out of the way by others, surprise him or her with a small portion of your tips for the night. Same thing with the bartender or host/hostess. This will reward you in dividends by rewarding the right behavior. They can sabotage or help you. Learn to influence them with your behavior and some money ... when they deserve it.

CONCLUSION

My father, John J. Turner, was born in Chrisman, Illinois, in 1922 to a family of poor sharecroppers. Living through the Depression, my dad hated being a farmer, and he especially hated being poor. He left the farm as soon as he graduated from high school, making his way to Indianapolis. He got a job in an Allis-Chalmers factory making farm machinery. Then came the Second World War, after which he returned to Allis-Chalmers and met my mother.

When my parents moved to Chicago so my dad could partner with his uncle in a cab company, my dad worked 120 hours his first week. However, he soon gave up his partnership and decided not to drive a cab for a living. After a few years, my dad got a job with the Chicago Public Works Department, then the Ford Motor Airplane Engine Company, located on the south side of Chicago, which had been reopened to build airplane engines for the Korean War.

Soon after, my dad got a job in the company's x-ray department inspecting airplane engine parts that were cast in metal. He and another guy who worked there bought a used x-ray machine and rented a dilapidated building next to the city dump in Blue Island, Illinois, a south Chicago suburb near 127th Street. My dad and his friend got some jobs inspecting metal castings from some other factories on the south side, completing the work at night and on weekends while working at Ford during the day.

When Ford closed its airplane engine division, my dad and his partner were given their pink slips but kept their side business, struggling to survive for years. Then, in about 1965, my dad bought out his partner and ran the company for years. He also started another company called Hydra Stop Inc., which my dad sold in 1993 before retiring.

What's the point of me telling you this story? Opportunity and success! It's about starting small and making it financially, about American opportunity. It's about you starting out as a server and using this profession as your springboard to financial success.

Think about it: quality servers are always in demand. You can and may need to start at a very low-end restaurant if you have no experience. But if you are motivated to work and educate yourself, you can and will prepare yourself to move up in the world. The goal is to work at a restaurant where most of the clientele are wealthy or at least doing pretty well financially. *You are never going to get rich serving poor people.*

So, how do you get there? It takes time. It takes effort. It takes vision. It takes planning and self-education.

Always do your employers right. You will need good references to get to work in the best places in town.

Finally, you will have the experience, skills, knowledge, and references to make it to one of the best restaurants in town, where you can really make money. Don't be afraid. You can do it, or at least you can try.

A high-end restaurant may be somewhere you may want to work for the rest of your life, but even if it isn't, it can be a springboard, helping you pursue other interests during the day.

Time Is Money

Most importantly, when you start making more money, don't become a consumer; become a saver and investor. Learn productive things you can do with your money. The biggest killer of your money 90 percent of the time is you. When most people begin to make a little money, they decide to spend it on clothes, shoes, makeup, video games, furniture, cars, consumables, cable TV, etc. Stop spending your money on things that start depreciating in value instantly.

Instead, open a high-yield savings account that pays better interest without a monthly or annual service fee. Set aside some money every time you get paid. Learn how to invest or how you can start a part-time business.

An Important Note about Investing

It is almost too easy to make mistakes when you first start investing. Let's say you want to invest in the stock market, mutual funds, or in physical gold or silver and eventually real estate. All of these things can be a great investment, but many first-time investors buy the right things at the wrong time or the wrong place.

You need to buy low and sell high, or at least buy when an asset is in the middle of its value cycle. Prices of most assets go up and down in value, depending on the strength or weakness of the economy or based on the demand (or lack thereof) of the asset. So, go slow and pay attention to market trends. No one can predict what's going to happen in the future, but be cautious and mindful. Make small investments that garner you either small gains or small losses. Buy assets that appreciate now and in the future.

Not only that, but invest time in learning and growing. Learn about the economy, the stock market, gold and silver, business logistics, bookkeeping, marketing, real estate investing, etc. Work for someone part time in a field you have always had an interest in. The possibilities are endless.

This is a short list of part-time roles you can start in: party planner, social media guru, copywriter, collectibles trader, car or boat reseller, eBay seller, house rehabber, website developer, home landscaper, podcaster, property manager, estate salesperson, handyman servicer, interior designer, mover, house painter, home inspector, domain seller, music instructor, jewelry maker, athletic trainer, pool cleaner, clothing alternator, child care provider, Amazon reseller, freelance writer, editor, graphic designer, online course educator, remote English teacher, SAT tutor, Etsy store owner, etc. Use your imagination and follow your interests. Invest in yourself and your future.

Have a Plan. Have a Vision. Have a Goal.

Failure is nothing more than a chance to revise your strategy.
— Anonymous

I have never been able to have a plan that worked out perfectly, and most of the time, I don't establish in my mind or write down exactly what my goals are in life or in business. But I have always had some sort of picture in my mind. Many would call it a vision of where I would like to be in the future.

George Washington Carver once said, "Where there is no vision, there is no hope." Hope is one of the foundations for motivation and perseverance, because making progress in life and in finances is hard. You will make many mistakes, but you need to keep trying. Having a vision helps you face uncertainty and failure, both of which are part of ultimately succeeding.

Being a server can be the beginning of years of financial success or a jumping-off point to almost any other type of life. Get a vision of what you would like to be or become, and with prayer to God, go for it. Go slow, be prudent, but get going. Use this book and your profession as a server as the beginning of the rest of your life.

SOME FINAL THOUGHTS

I've given you some practical suggestions in this book. The establishment where you work probably has some practical procedures you are required to follow, but what they probably haven't taught you is how to connect with your customers and keep them relaxed and enjoying their time and meal.

Establish contact with your customers as soon as you can. This can be eye contact with a hand signal, but get there as soon as you can and introduce yourself, telling them your name. See what they want to drink and find out how quickly they want to order. Some people are in a hurry and some people are there to take their time and enjoy the evening and the event. Proceed accordingly.

Pay attention and look at your customers every time you are on the dining floor. If the opportunity arises when you are serving their meal, mention the phenomenal after-dinner drinks and desserts on hand. This is a great way to "whet their appetite," so to speak, but don't go into too many details all at once. See if the customer seems interested and follow his or her lead. Do the same with the dessert menu.

Watch and see when they look like they are ready to go. Customers are very fickle at this time. This is when they will ultimately decide what your tip will be, so make sure they're not waiting. Get their bill to them as soon as you can.

As for the customer connection, try to think about the orchestra analogy I mentioned before. The conductor is the leader. Whatever the conductor directs, he or she gets from the musicians, but the musicians must always be paying attention to the conductor. As a waiter, you can't possibly be at every table all the time. The trick is the connection: stay connected through eye contact and nonverbal communication. When you establish this connection, your customers know they can and will get your attention quickly because they know you are constantly looking and communicating with them from afar.

Never interrupt if your customer is talking. I was at a restaurant today while editing this chapter. The waitress was great. She was friendly, personable, diligent, and timely, but she interrupted every time she came to our table. She was only trying to make sure we had everything we needed. But she did not care or think about the fact that we were talking. One time she came to our table and interrupted us by asking, "Do you have everything you need?" We of course had to stop what we were talking about so we could answer her question. I then watched her go to every one of her tables and interrupt every single table she was waiting on.

Just walk close to the table and everyone will see you. If they want something, they will say so. If not, back away and move on.

Try to make their night memorable. Offer them some great desserts or after-dinner drinks. Make sure you do not make them wait at the beginning or end of the meal. Make sure to tell them "thank you."

Moving up to better and more expensive restaurants is the way to make more money. This is probably a scary thought for most people. In the real world, there is usually a connection between risk and reward. If you stay where you are, there may not be much risk, but there also isn't much reward.

Prepare yourself. Study and continue to learn more about serving, wines, and drinks. This will build your confidence. Then, talk with someone at a better restaurant about a job.

If you implement these ideas, you will shine, and in time, you will "double your tips." I guarantee it.

CHECKLIST TO KEEP YOU ON TRACK

1. Make eye contact with all of your new customers as soon as they sit down. Make a signal or a head nod to let them know you saw them. Then they can relax.
2. Get to new customers' tables ASAP and introduce yourself.
3. Always keep in mind *why* people dine out.
4. Follow the customers' lead.
5. Mention dessert and after-dinner drinks early.
6. Never interrupt a customer.
7. Learn about table etiquette, after-dinner drinks, and desserts.
8. Look at the people at every table every time you are on the dining floor.
9. *Soon* is better than *wait*.
10. Never make them wait. Stay connected by using eye contact and body language.
11. Be on the dining floor looking, signaling, and serving.

12. Make your customers' night memorable.
13. Mention dessert again at the end of the meal.
14. Tell each customer which copy of the bill is his or hers.
15. Make sure to say "thank you."
16. Prepare yourself for bigger and better restaurants.
17. If you are not at the best place, then go apply for a job serving at a better restaurant.
18. Don't be afraid; overcome your fear. Go get that better job.

Appendix A

MONEY-BACK GUARANTEE

The guarantee implied in the title of this book is based on the presumption that the purchaser is a server and will implement these ideas and practices for a period of at least six months. If, after implementing these ideas and practices for six months, the purchaser is dissatisfied, he or she will be eligible for a full refund.

There are two requirements for your money back.

1. First send a copy of proof of purchase with the date on the receipt along with a written request for a full refund to Jim Turner, 111 Isle Creek Drive, Memphis, TN 38103.

2. Send a copy of your current payroll receipt proving you work at a restaurant along with your correct name and return address.

Appendix B

TEST YOUR KNOWLEDGE

Double Your Tips: Test

Let's see if you know what you need to "Double Your Tips."

This test can be self-administered or used by restaurant managers or owners to test a server's knowledge and understanding of being a server.

1. **Why do most people go out to eat?**
   a. Because they want to spend a lot of money.
   b. Because it's the cool thing to do.
   c. To be with friends, a date, to celebrate a special event, to entertain a client, etc.
   d. To get away from people.

2. **What four-letter word does your customer not want to hear or experience?**
   a. Gift
   b. Fast
   c. Wait
   d. Nice

3. **What is nonverbal communication?**
   a. A CIA Secret?
   b. Communicating to someone by using your eyes, hands, fingers, head, face, or body.
   c. A modern technology.
   d. Something only children use to communicate.

4. What are examples of nonverbal communication?

   a. Looking at all of your customers every time you walk on to the dining floor.

   b. Looking at your customers and giving them a hand signal.

   c. When your customers look at you and you nod your head at them.

   d. All of the above.

5. When should you not look at your customer?

   a. When he is putting food in his mouth.

   b. When he is taking a drink.

   c. When he is talking to someone at his table.

   d. Always look at your customers even if you are busy. You can at least give them a head nod or a hand signal so they can relax and know you have seen they need you.

6. Is there ever a time when you should not talk to your customers?

   a. Never, they need to talk to first. You are busy.

   b. Who do they think they are making you wait for them?

   c. When you walk up to their table and they are talking and don't acknowledge you, back away and go to another customer's table.

   d. Talk loudly over your customers' conversation and ask them if they need anything.

7. **Should you ever interrupt your customers when they are talking?**

   a. Yes, anytime you want to.
   b. Yes, if they want their food quickly, they need to stop what they are doing and talk with you.
   c. Yes, especially when they might look like they are proposing marriage or something like that.
   d. No, look at your customers' table, and walk up to your customers' table. Let them see you wait a few seconds. If they don't look or talk to you, back away.

8. **When is the most important time in your customers' experience?**

   a. All the time. You should spend all of your time on them and forget about your other customers.
   b. When the food is served.
   c. When customers are first seated at their table. They need to know that someone knows they are there and they will be attended to shortly, if not immediately. Then they can relax and socialize or enjoy the entertainment.
   d. When their first drinks are delivered to their table.

9. **When is the second most important time in your customers' experience?**

   a. When they get their menus.
   b. Near the end of your customers' meal. If everything has gone well, you need a smooth landing. When your customers are finished or finishing, do not rush them. But don't make them wait when it is time for them to give you your tip.
   c. When you see anyone go to the restroom.
   d. When your customers receive their food order.

10. **Is repeat business good for you as a waiter and for the restaurant?**

   a. Good food and good service makes people want to come back to your restaurant.
   b. You want people to come back to your restaurant and you want them to ask for you to be their server.
   c. Repeat business and customers is the key to any restaurant's success and yours also. If the restaurant prospers, so will you.
   d. All of the above.

11. Is understanding table etiquette important for a server?

    a. No, that is just old-fashioned stuff.

    b. Yes, many people use table etiquette to signal that they are not finished or they are finished eating. Understanding table etiquette can increase your skills as a server and your tips.

    c. Never heard of that kind of stuff.

    d. All of the above.

12. How is it possible to help your customers create a memory while dining at your restaurant?

    a. By suggesting foods, drinks, and desserts that create a sight, smell, and taste experience.

    b. By giving them a card.

    c. By singing to them.

    d. None of the above.

13. Why should you know especially about the after-dinner drinks your restaurant offers?

    a. Knowing what your restaurant offers is part of being a good server.

    b. Drinks, especially after-dinner drinks, can be a wonderful experience for your customers and help to create a memory using the sight, smell, and taste of something unique.

c. It is a great thing to do for your customers and will increase your tips. It is a mutual benefit for your customers and you.

d. All of the above.

14. When should you mention the great desserts you have at the restaurant?

a. At the end of the meal when your customers are ready for their check.

b. As soon as possible in your interaction with your customers. Quickly mention the great desserts available at your restaurant so your customers can think about dessert and save room for dessert.

c. After you have brought them their check.

d. Before you ask them if they want something to drink.

15. When should you pay attention to your customers?

a. Only when they first sit down.

b. Only at the beginning and the end of their meal.

c. From beginning to the end. The beginning and the ending are the most important, but staying in contact with your customers through verbal and nonverbal communication must be maintained every time you are on the dining floor.

d.   Only when you have time to talk with them.

16. Why is it important to you as a server to have good relationships with other restaurant employees?

a.   It does not matter. Just take care of your customers.

b.   Many of the other employees can sink your ship. The host or hostess can send all of the bad customers to your tables, the bartender can make your drink orders last, and the cook can do the same. Take care of these people with praise, compliments, and sometimes part of your tips.

c.   Because then they will be your friend.

d.   All of the above.

17. Is it important to spend time on the dining floor area?

a.   No, when you get caught up, hang around the kitchen and in the back with the other servers.

b.   Yes, you need to be where you can see your customers.

c.   No, you need to rest between trips to the dining floor.

d.   All of the above.

18. If you begin to make more and more money as a server, what should you do with all of that money?

    a.   Save all of the money you can.

    b.   Save that money for a rainy day.

    c.   Spend all the money you can.

    d.   Both a & b above.

19. Why should you tell your customers "thank you" when you give them the check?

    a.   Saying "thank you" is stupid. They should be thanking you. You did all of the work.

    b.   Your customer selected the restaurant you work at. They did not have to come to your restaurant and you want them to come back. And they gave you an opportunity to serve them, and if you did a really good job, they will probably give you a good tip.

    c.   Because that is what your mother taught you to do.

    d.   Because your boss will be mad if you don't.

20. Why should you do all of this work for these people that have more money than you?

a. Because working as a server is an honorable profession.

b. Because that is how it works. You give and then others will give to you.

c. Because you will please both yourself and others.

d. All of the above.

Appendix C

TEST KEY

1. **Why do most people go out to eat?**

   a. Because they want to spend a lot of money.
   b. Because it's the cool thing to do.
   c. To be with friends, a date, to celebrate a special event, to entertain a client, etc.
   d. To get away from people.

2. **What four-letter word does your customer not want to hear or experience?**

   a. Gift
   b. Fast
   c. Wait
   d. Nice

3. **What is nonverbal communication?**

   a. A CIA Secret?
   b. Communicating to someone by using your eyes, hands, fingers, head, face, or body.
   c. A modern technology.
   d. Something only children use to communicate.

4. **What are examples of nonverbal communication?**

   a. Looking at all of your customers every time you walk on to the dining floor.

   b. Looking at your customers and giving them a hand signal.

   c. When your customers look at you and you nod your head at them.

   d. All of the above.

5. **When should you not look at your customer?**

   a. When he is putting food in his mouth.

   b. When he is taking a drink.

   c. When he is talking to someone at his table.

   d. Always look at your customers even if you are busy. You can at least give them a head nod or a hand signal so they can relax and know you have seen they need you.

6. **Is there ever a time when you should not talk to your customers?**

   a. Never, they need to talk to first. You are busy.

   b. Who do they think they are making you wait for them?

   c. When you walk up to their table and they are talking and don't acknowledge you, back away and go to another customer's table.

   d. Talk loudly over your customers' conversation and ask them if they need anything.

7. **Should you ever interrupt your customers when they are talking?**

   a. Yes, anytime you want to.
   b. Yes, if they want their food quickly, they need to stop what they are doing and talk with you.
   c. Yes, especially when they might look like they are proposing marriage or something like that.
   d. No, look at your customers' table, and walk up to your customers' table. Let them see you wait a few seconds. If they don't look or talk to you, back away.

8. **When is the most important time in your customers' experience?**

   a. All the time. You should spend all of your time on them and forget about your other customers.
   b. When the food is served.
   c. When customers are first seated at their table. They need to know that someone knows they are there and they will be attended to shortly, if not immediately. Then they can relax and socialize or enjoy the entertainment.
   d. When their first drinks are delivered to their table.

9. **When is the second most important time in your customers' experience?**

   a. When they get their menus.

   b. Near the end of your customers' meal. If everything has gone well, you need a smooth landing. When your customers are finished or finishing, do not rush them. But don't make them wait when it is time for them to give you your tip.

   c. When you see anyone go to the restroom.

   d. When your customers receive their food order.

10. **Is repeat business good for you as a waiter and for the restaurant?**

   a. Good food and good service makes people want to come back to your restaurant.

   b. You want people to come back to your restaurant and you want them to ask for you to be their server.

   c. Repeat business and customers is the key to any restaurant's success and yours also. If the restaurant prospers, so will you.

   d. All of the above.

11. Is understanding table etiquette important for a server?

a. No, that is just old-fashioned stuff.

b. Yes, many people use table etiquette to signal that they are not finished or they are finished eating. Understanding table etiquette can increase your skills as a server and your tips.

c. Never heard of that kind of stuff.

d. All of the above.

12. How is it possible to help your customers create a memory while dining at your restaurant?

a. By suggesting foods, drinks, and desserts that create a sight, smell, and taste experience.

b. By giving them a card.

c. By singing to them.

d. None of the above.

13. Why should you know especially about the after-dinner drinks your restaurant offers?

a. Knowing what your restaurant offers is part of being a good server.

b. Drinks, especially after-dinner drinks, can be a wonderful experience for your customers and help to create a memory using the sight, smell, and taste of something unique.

c. It is a great thing to do for your customers and will increase your tips. It is a mutual benefit for your customers and you.

d. All of the above.

14. When should you mention the great desserts you have at the restaurant?

a. At the end of the meal when your customers are ready for their check.

b. As soon as possible in your interaction with your customers. Quickly mention the great desserts available at your restaurant so your customers can think about dessert and save room for dessert.

c. After you have brought them their check.

d. Before you ask them if they want something to drink.

15. When should you pay attention to your customers?

a. Only when they first sit down.

b. Only at the beginning and the end of their meal.

c. From beginning to the end. The beginning and the ending are the most important, but staying in contact with your customers through verbal and nonverbal communication must be maintained every time you are on the dining floor.

    d.   Only when you have time to talk with them.

16. Why is it important to you as a server to have good relationships with other restaurant employees?

    a.   It does not matter. Just take care of your customers.

    b.   Many of the other employees can sink your ship. The host or hostess can send all of the bad customers to your tables, the bartender can make your drink orders last, and the cook can do the same. Take care of these people with praise, compliments, and sometimes part of your tips.

    c.   Because then they will be your friend.

    d.   All of the above.

17. Is it important to spend time on the dining floor area?

    a.   No, when you get caught up, hang around the kitchen and in the back with the other servers.

    b.   Yes, you need to be where you can see your customers.

    c.   No, you need to rest between trips to the dining floor.

    d.   All of the above.

18. If you begin to make more and more money as a server, what should you do with all of that money?

    a.   Save all of the money you can.

    b.   Save that money for a rainy day.

    c.   Spend all the money you can.

    d.   Both a & b above.

19. Why should you tell your customers "thank you" when you give them the check?

    a.   Saying "thank you" is stupid. They should be thanking you. You did all of the work.

    b.   Your customer selected the restaurant you work at. They did not have to come to your restaurant and you want them to come back. And they gave you an opportunity to serve them, and if you did a really good job, they will probably give you a good tip.

    c.   Because that is what your mother taught you to do.

    d.   Because your boss will be mad if you don't.

20. Why should you do all of this work for these people that have more money than you?

a. Because working as a server is an honorable profession.

b. Because that is how it works. You give and then others will give to you.

c. Because you will please both yourself and others.

d. All of the above.

IF YOU ENJOYED THIS BOOK, WILL YOU HELP ME SPREAD THE WORD?

There are several ways you can help me get the word out about the message of this book...

- Post a 5-Star review on Amazon.
- Write about the book on your Facebook, Twitter, Instagram, LinkedIn—any social media you regularly use!
- If you blog, consider referencing the book, or publishing an excerpt from the book with a link back to my website. You have my permission to do this if you provide proper credit and backlinks.
- Recommend the book to friends—word-of-mouth is still the most effective form of advertising.
- Purchase additional copies to give away as gifts.

The best way to connect is by sending me an email: doubleyourtips6@gmail.com

Published by HigherLife Development Services Inc.
PO Box 623307
Oviedo, Florida 32762
www.ahigherlife.com

Paperback ISBN: 978-1-958211-78-6
Ebook ISBN: 978-1-958211-79-3

Printed in USA
For more details on the money-back guarantee, refer to Appendix A.

www.ingramcontent.com/pod-product-compliance
Lightning Source LLC
Chambersburg PA
CBHW071709210326
41597CB00017B/2404